Definitely TRUE
YEAR ONE

A collection of lies from Jason van Gumster
M. J. GUNS

THE GIANT COFFEE BLUNDERBUSS

Definitely True: Year One — A Collection of Lies from Jason van Gumster

M. J. Guns

Copyright © 2015 M. J. Guns. All rights reserved.

Published by The Giant Coffee Blunderbuss
ISBN 978-1-943474-00-4

To you. Be careful what you ask for.

Continue following new lies each and every day at definitelytrue.com.

Also, while you're there, feel free to subscribe to the mailing list so you can stay up to date with recommendations, future books of lies, and other writings by M. J. Guns. Maybe you could even suggest a future lie!

Based on a true story.

(Hint: You can read through these lies sequentially, but if you go to the back, there's a super-helpful index. Just sayin'.)

Lie 1

Fetal pigs carry a unique strain of rabies that causes victims to chew off their three outermost toes while chirping like a baby crow. The disease can only be cured by placing the victim in a jar of formaldehyde for up to thirty-six hours.

Lie 2

Airplanes were originally designed as subterranean vehicles. In the late 1800s, there was a huge interest in underground travel as a faster, safer means of transit. The idea was to develop a needle-shaped craft that could, in essence, be injected into the Earth's crust to the fluid layers beneath. There would be multiple injection/extraction hubs that would allow these vehicles to enter and exit transit space.

The first test hubs were placed near fault lines and volcanoes, where access to the sub-crust layer is easiest. Well, as fate would have it, there was an accident at on of the original testing zones in southern Montana. During an extraction test, one of the transit needles was launched into the sky from an overload of sub-surface back-pressure.

This had happened before, but there was a guy in attendance for the test named Fredrick Caulton. He observed that as the launched needle went through the air, it seemed to stay aloft longer than it should have. This had something to do with the shape of the solidified lava on the control surfaces of the needle. He took a sample of this to his home town of Dayton, Ohio for further tests. He had an apartment over a bike shop…

Lie 3

The western coast of the Bering Strait is made out of chocolate.

Lie 4

Stepping on a crack in the sidewalk will, in fact, cause you to break your back. This is because of a unique property of concrete wherein subsonic pulses emanate from the surface when pressure is applied to a fault. These pulses disrupt the equilibrium of humans, causing them to fall and potentially cause severe damage to their spinal column.

Lie 5

The state of Wyoming is the result of a large conspiracy to commit a bad practical joke on former president Grover Cleveland.

Lie 6

Remy Johnston, renowned underwater tournament yo-yo champion and pole vaulter, was the first person to ever successfully skip his own body across Lake Mead.

Lie 7

Early humans were practically unchokeable. What is now the common human sternum was once a bony face shield that protected the throats of Cro-Magnon man from various attackers. It is commonly believed that this trait receded quickly because it was nearly impossible for people to see around this bone shield, so they removed it along with the head that it was protecting… "just in case."

Lie 8

The McDonnell Douglas AV-8B was originally named the Woolly Mammoth, the nickname of the hair-covered test pilot that first flew it. However, the marketing department of McDonnell Douglas wanted something that sounded faster. After 13 weeks of debate, they settled on the current common name, the Harrier.

Lie 9

In Collinsworth, Kentucky, all forms of expression are legally required to be expressed as a value in units of "awesomesauce." The only exception to this dictate is when describing the quality of any particular sauce. In those cases, the use of "awesome" is forbidden, as doing so would cause confusion.

Lie 10

The carrier pigeon gets its name from the fact that while in flight, it can launch a small squad of smaller pigeons from its back to attack neighboring crow airbases.

Lie 11

The lettuce "plant" is not actually a plant. Each head of lettuce is actually a single cell in a multi-lettuce organism that survives by slowly devouring the Earth's core.

Lie 12

Dr. Seuss's *The Cat in the Hat* was a story based on his obese 3rd-grade teacher whom he remembers very little of, other than her strange hats and uncontrollable facial hair.

Lie 13

14 out of every 17 doorknobs that you touch have been pooped on by birds.

Lie 14

The "burger" part of the words "hamburger" and "cheeseburger" was originally supposed to be "surger" as a marketing term to let the beef industry compete with a growing energy bar industry. Unfortunately, when trying to describe things that taste like ground-beef sandwiches, people said things tasted "ham-surgery" or "cheese-surgery," inspiring visions of dissected pigs and cheese. The problem was alleviated when a secretary made a typo in a memo to the Beef Production Association's Board of Advisers.

Lie 15

Martin Short was actually shot and killed during the filming of *The Three Amigos*. Jim Henson created the first robotic Muppet as a permanent stand-in to keep audiences unaware of the truth. To this day, the Muppet of Martin Short still successfully pulls off its impersonation, fooling audiences all over the world.

Lie 16

There was a fad in Hollywood in the 1980's that had all the stars getting intensive plastic surgery to appear vertically stretched. This was done so they could match their stretched appearance once their movies hit video tape. The advent of pan and scan technologies that removed the "stretchiness" in non-widescreen video removed the need for such surgery. Unfortunately, reversing the process for each of Hollywood's stars has not been as simple.

Lie 17

The zipper was originally a cruel invention designed to frustrate a rising class of discontent handbag factory laborers.

Lie 18

Of the original "California Raisins" singing group that was so popular in the mid 1990s, 3 were actually prunes.

Lie 19

Jack the Ripper was actually a copycat murderer. He caught on better with the media, though, for his flashier name. Norton the Creepy Guy with a Knife Behind You simply didn't sell newspapers like Jack could.

Lie 20

It is a well know fact by physicists that the faster you move, the larger and more shock absorbent the objects around you become. This is easily illustrated by driving a car into a concrete wall at over 150 miles per hour. Note how quickly the car ceases to move and how difficult it was to avoid the wall.

Lie 21

Humans do not actually have a pinky finger. It is the product of a mass conspiracy to brainwash the populace into believing that they have more functionality than they really do. Your pinky finger does not exist in reality, kind of like baseball.

Lie 22

In the event of suffocation due to violent strangulation, your best recourse is to deflate a rubber balloon into your ear. The Eustachian tube is actually an emergency snorkel for the lungs. This is an effective means of activating it.

Lie 23

What kind of plant a seed comes from doesn't determine what it grows into. This is actually determined by writing the name of the plant you'd like to grow on a short strip of masking tape folded around a toothpick. Place this in the soil next to the seed you plant and what you've written on the tape will grow from that spot. It's true. Gardeners do it all the time.

Lie 24

Pushpins were originally developed as silent blow-dart weapons for Nazi Germany. In a strange mission-gone-awry, one of the operators of this weapon missed his target, a highly ranked officer in the Icelandic Marines. The trajectorily askew dart ripped a piece of paper out of the officer's hand and stuck it to the wall. This has lead to the common misconception that the pushpin was developed in Iceland.

Lie 25

Thumbtacks, on the other hand, were entirely developed in Iceland.

Lie 26

February actually has 30 full days in it. However, you never notice it because they sneak by when you're sleeping. If you manage to stay awake for the entire month, you'll actually experience all thirty days in it.

Lie 27

The ostrich can run at 3 times the speed of light. However, the entire species has an innate understanding of the ramifications that this imposes on the space-time continuum, so they rarely ever do it. Those that do are so overwhelmed by the brightness and energy of superluminous travel that they stick their heads in the ground to dampen the shock to their systems.

Lie 28

Unlike cartoons, which can inflate their heads by blowing on their thumbs, when regular people blow on their thumbs, they only inflate their pinky.

Lie 29

It takes precisely 438 bottle-rockets to get the State of Rhode Island to escape velocity (that is, the velocity an object must be going in order to escape the Earth's gravitational pull and achieve orbit).

Lie 30

The Earth's core is 70% composed of jellybeans. The remaining 30% is equal parts jawbreakers and dryer lint.

Lie 31

The origin of the word "fetus" comes from the ancient belief that prior to birth, babies don't have feet. They sit in the womb their full term and when they're ready to be born, they telepathically contact their mother. Unborn babies share a hive mind, so when they contact a particular mother to give birth, they speak in plural when referring to themselves. And they don't specifically declare that one of them is ready to be born. They request feet, saying, "Feet us." This causes the mother to induce labor, giving birth to an individual child, complete with feet.

Lie 32

The pterodactyl's diet consisted entirely of sand and formaldehyde. This is what kept their remains intact for the millions of years until humans discovered them and wore them as funny hats.

Lie 33

Polynesian cows have a 73% greater chance of getting inverted nipples than both European and American cows.

Lie 34

The world only exists as you consciously perceive it. In fact, when you fall asleep, the world ceases to exist. Things appear to have happened while you sleep only because the human mind cannot understand instant discontinuities in time. This also applies to seeing people who are sleeping. They are not actually there. They've blinked out of existence, but your mind has retained an image of their shell prior to their disappearance.

Neat, huh?

Lie 35

The "lens flare" is the most respected and complicated visual effect in all media. It's a good idea to use it whenever possible… especially in logos.

Lie 36

Feral brain slugs have taken over the minds of 19% of the world's leaders. Together, they are planning to rid the earth of all salt, ushering in the rule of the slugs and enslaving all of mankind.

Lie 37

According to the 7th Black Book of Tolbathlan, a cursed spirit can be forced to dance an Irish jig by chanting the lyrics to "Camptown Races" for 45 minutes.

Lie 38

The reason for the "don't feed the animals" signs at zoos has nothing to do with protecting you *or* the diet of the animals. It's because usually the food that's given to zoo animals is candy and zoo administration don't want their animals developing a brand loyalty and endorsing products that they don't approve of.

Lie 39

Chickens taste like peanut butter.

Lie 40

The painting on the ceiling of the Sistine Chapel is actually wallpaper… cheap wallpaper.

Lie 41

There is nothing to fear on the Ides of March... especially if you're an ancient Roman ruler with a good friend named Brutus.

Lie 42

The fast-forward button on most tape decks and VCRs these days was originally called the "wind" button to correspond with the rewind button. However, in the first test versions of tape decks, the manufacturing crew misunderstood the pronunciation of that button, so early prototypes had large fans attached to them that would turn on and blow air into your face each time you wanted to move through the video quickly.

Lie 43

There will be no lies today.

Lie 44

The North American Circus Clown has been listed as the world's most elusive animal. This is mainly for the creatures ingenious camouflage. By appearing in the most brightly non-matching garb, it stuns other animals into what can only be described as a stark disbelief. Clowns are such an eye-sore that all animals, including most humans, will not allow themselves to believe that what they are seeing is there, and because of this, the existence of the clown is not perceived.

There's probably one sitting next to you right now.

Lie 45

The stomach of the ancient mastodon was coated with a rough concoction not unlike what you get when you mix sugar with Velveeta cheese.

Lie 46

James Kingswell, a high school teacher in the late 1930s was the first person on record to be able to lick his own eyebrow.

Lie 47

Being late for anything more than two times in a row causes a temporal shift in the space-time continuum that results in the abrupt death of some child's pet gerbil.

Lie 48

The "dunce cap" originally had a practical purpose outside of simply drawing attention to the person designated as the dunce. Dunce-like behavior was believed to have been caused by an overheated mind. The initial solution to this was to stick an ice cream cone (with ice cream) upside-down upon the overly warm surface.

Lie 49

In literature, the term "heroine" refers to a strong, heroic female lead character. This is derived from the superhuman strength that medieval women used to get from their opium-laced make-up.

Lie 50

The tune to the now infamous "Hamster Dance" was previously used by the National Elevator Test Bureau to determine how quickly an annoying sound in a confined space would cause a person to self-destructively snap. The average time was 12 minutes.

Lie 51

Cardiac arrest is kind of like house arrest, except it involves playing poker with water buffalo without cheating.

Oh… and your face explodes, too.

Lie 52

45% of the time, when someone wishes upon a star, they're actually wishing upon a planet.

Lie 53

Pigeons, the roaming piranha of the sky, attack their unaware victims without warning, lifting them into the sky and picking their bones clean before they reach a 50-foot altitude. In large cities, pigeon swarms can get as large as 1000 individual birds and can average 15-30 abductions a day.

Lie 54

According to VanStanzberg's *New Anatomy*, the pelvis is actually arranged improperly in most skeletons (both inanimate models and the one under your skin). It's actually supposed to be upside down from it's current configuration.

Lie 55

Approximately 44 hamsters died in their hamster wheels in order to transmit this message to your computer.

Lie 56

The approximate numerical value of "forever" is 400 divided by 12.

Lie 57

You can tell the difference between a whether a duck is alive or dead by poking it with a stick. The living duck will have Jell-o ooze from its wings.

Lie 58

There was recently a push to change April Fool's Day to April's Food Day by renowned East Alaskan chef April O'Learysmith. It nearly passed a with a vote in Montana, but everyone in the Montana state government thought the idea was a joke and didn't actually show up to vote.

Lie 59

To more easily catch its prey, the peregrine falcon can fly backwards, so its silhouette more closely resembles that of a non-predatory bird to animals on the ground.

Lie 60

George Washington's fake teeth were made out of the wood from the cherry tree he cut down.

Lie 61

It is virtually impossible to tear Canadian money. This is because it's made with the first truly synthetic silk and is 45 times stronger than Kevlar, steel, and titanium. Canadians have been known to tie bills together to make a kind of rope to use for holding things together, stating that "it works way better than duct tape."

Lie 62

Flying fish developed the ability to fly in an attempt at capturing what they believed to be their primary prey, the "dry sponge." Unfortunately, what they called dry sponges are actually clouds and the refractive nature of the water's surface made them seem much closer than they actually are.

Lie 63

The national anthem of Panama is a Spanish version of "Row, Row, Row Your Boat."

Lie 64

To the contrary, One (1) is not the loneliest number. It's actually just the quietest number. 73 is really the loneliest number.

Lie 65

Jefferson Sheldon Sumpter Cates-Ford Henderson Smith of Holland, Michigan is the only person to date to have 7 surnames in his full name.

Lie 66

The marmoset is the only animal capable of flinging itself through the air like a Frisbee. Flying squirrels came close, but gave up before perfecting the technique.

Lie 67

Hugh Doggs of Winchester, Nebraska is responsible for naming 42 of the 67 classifications of toenail clippings. A birth defect left him with 16 toes on each foot, so, in his words, he's "kind of like an Eskimo is with snow... only in this case, it's with toenails."

Lie 68

The CEO of Ford had his dog appointed to the company's board of advisers for a week.

Lie 69

Every time a sheep defecates, it creates a pristine alternate reality enclosed in its feces.

Lie 70

Studies have shown that travel by slingshot is 26% more efficient than travel by public transit.

Lie 71

At first glance, being pushed down a flight of stairs and falling down a mountain may appear to be similar. However, they are not. The former allows you to transcend the reality of your plight by forcing you to hum the tune to "3 Blind Mice" as you fall.

Lie 72

Prolonged exposure to cellular phones will empower you with the gift of flight.

Lie 73

The kilt was actually designed as a mini-skirt. However, being ahead of its time and destined to be worn by women, the design was modified to include a lengthened cut, pleats, and plaid.

Lie 74

The next day does not start until you go to sleep and wake up again.

Lie 75

Moles have perfectly functioning eyes that see better than those of most predators. However, the muscles that control their eyelids are inoperable. This prevents them from using their eyes and has lead to the misconception that they are blind.

Lie 76

The wheel was never really invented. People have always had wheels. The real breakthrough invention was the axle.

Lie 77

Lawn darts are one of the few remaining artifacts that reveal the existence of an ancient race of giants.

Lie 78

Even leopards think that their fur pattern is tacky.

Lie 79

Tennis and badminton both originated as games played by house servants charged with the responsibility of taking care of the family cat. Both the tennis ball and the shuttlecock were originally large hairballs.

Lie 80

Contrary to popular belief, giraffes did not evolve long necks from a need to reach food in higher places. They've always had long necks. This was an advantage when they were a tree-dwelling species, swinging their bodies from branch to branch in the jungle by biting them with their smooth, rounded teeth and abnormally intense jaw strength.

Lie 81

Recursive: Like cursive, only twice as annoying to read.

Lie 82

Horses have a hidden beak behind their teeth that they use for tearing the flesh off of unsuspecting prey that hold apples too near to their faces.

Lie 83

Tomatoes are neither fruits nor vegetables. They are the heads of a miniature race of children bent on total world domination.

Lie 84

Chairs are an ancient alien race of "L"-shaped creatures that live on the flesh of humans. There have been no recent attacks because the chair species only has to eat every 500 years. They are simply waiting. 7 months to go.

Lie 85

Goats have no problems re-entering Earth's atmosphere from orbit because their hooves are heat-shielded.

Lie 86

Temporary tattoos are chemical mind-control agents devised by an underground network of sophisticated jewel thieves and farmers.

Lie 87

It's mathematically impossible to clap your feet together and make it sound like it was really your hands.

Lie 88

Driving a car in reverse *really* fast will, in fact, send you back in time. Unfortunately, everyone who has tried this has run into a wall and knocked themselves unconscious until they wake up in present day.

Lie 89

Parakeets are the subliminal mind-control agents of an underground race of psychokinetic super-beings. They act as remote transmission stations designed to enhance the range of these beings, who are made of pudding and are therefore immobile.

Lie 90

Punctuation is never really necessary for written communication. It eventually gets worked out because people will call you on the phone and ask you what you wrote anyway. When they do that, make sure that you stutter and slur your words as much as possible… because proper enunciation is never really necessary for verbal communication.

Lie 91

All horses are named Frederick.

Lie 92

Unlike the rest of the ape-descendant human race, people from Portugal are actually a highly evolved descendant of a prehistoric species of goose called the Portchudon. In fact, that's where the name Portugal comes from... these Portudon Geese... or Portuguese.

Lie 93

Duke Nukem Forever will eventually hit stores... but it will be the real guy, not the game.

Lie 94

If you can manage to balance your entire body weight at the tip of your pinky finger, you aren't special at all. Everyone can do that.

Lie 95

The phrase "third time's a charm" is actually an expression that refers to one of the world's oldest unsolvable math problems. The problem is that no one knows the proper value for charm to multiply by one-third.

Lie 96

Facial twitching is a sign of nudity.

Lie 97

The oldest living human being is a Finnish man by the name of Bob Yodelman. He's 203 years old and still does 100 one-armed push-ups each day. His left arm is very weak.

Lie 98

Humans were meant to live underground and burrow holes to form a subteropolis name Rangaria. Unfortunately, the first humans never quite knew exactly how to follow orders.

Lie 99

The War of 1812 took place entirely within the confines of an intergalactic pinball machine.

Lie 100

Car dealers are the noblest form of human life.

Lie 101

Cannonballs were created on accident. The original design called for something more pyramid-shaped. However, when ridiculed for his idea, the designer took the tomatoes that were being thrown at him and fired them back at his critics. Seeing how well that worked, he later conceded that they were right.

Lie 102

According to the U.S. Copyright Office, methodologies for committing various crimes such as robbery, trespassing, indecent exposure, and public drunkenness are all prescribed actions that may be subject to copyright. Murder and extortion, however, are not subject to copyright, because it's so easy to do those crimes on accident.

Lie 103

The concept of "turning back time" only makes sense in the context of clocks. The true act of reversing time is more akin to making an origami frog.

Lie 104

Body odor is not a sign that you are dirty. Rather, it's a signal to your nervous system that otherworldly nanobots have infiltrated your body's level-one defenses and are proceeding to make their way to your central core.

Lie 105

The newest line of coffee-flavored mints from Flav-O-Mint have a two-part purpose:
1. It's a new product that they want to sell.
2. The CEO of Flav-O-Mint has naturally bad coffee breath and this is his attempt at trying to get people think that coffee breath "isn't all that bad."

Lie 106

Filing cabinets were first designed as a prison cell for renegade badgers.

Lie 107

If you run around in a circle with a 3-foot radius fast enough, you will quickly begin levitating. Unfortunately, the second that you realize that this is happening, you will come crashing back down to the ground. Many a person and dog have tragically perished due to this strange quirk in the laws of physics.

Lie 108

The word "supplemental" is statistically the most difficult to spell word in the English language... followed second by "statistically."

Lie 109

Compact Discs, or CDs, were originally created as military weapons. However, contrary to the common view, they weren't intended to be launchable discs. Rather, they were designed to capture the enemy's soul and trap it in a shimmering rainbow hell.

Lie 110

In Greenland, during the summer of 1962, there was a study to compare the verbal articulation of humans at 4:00 AM with that of ferrets at the same time of day. Ferrets were found to be superior in that regard.

Lie 111

Excessive usage of palindromes has been proven to cause people to have an unnecessary ambivalence to their lives.

Lie 112

The concept of the recursive acronym was first devised as a means of distracting elementary school students long enough to escape their evil clutches.

As evidenced by the Great Teacher Disappearance of 1864, it was unsuccessful at that.

Lie 113

According to ancient Greek legend, the 100-meter dash in the track & field events at the Olympics originally involved cadavers and maple syrup. Unfortunately, details are sketchy, since the only documented proof of this was etched into a half-eaten cookie that was preserved in tar.

Lie 114

The old Atari video game "Asteroids" was based on a true story… they just didn't know that at the time when they made it.

Lie 115

Despite the nomadic lifestyle of the blue and black variations of the North American Inkpen, or "cheap ballpoint," researchers have yet to discover why the various species have not cross-bred to create more variation in their species. The hope is to find a way to facilitate the evolution of a pen with unlimited ink.

Lie 116

Back pain is just another way of your body saying, "Hey, you're doing a great job!"

Lie 117

Chainmail was not, as is commonly believed, designed to protect the wearer from glancing enemy blows with sharp weapons. It was actually made as a torture device to weigh down the wearer, making him easier to catch for the attack dogs.

Lie 118

City governments take the appearance of their skylines very seriously. Abstract shapes at various heights and widths are a natural defense against killer bees.

Lie 119

Your skeleton is a uniquely shaped key to a transdimensional doorway. Unfortunately, the only way to use the key is to liberate it from the confines of your flesh and muscle… a process that is typically fatal in most climates.

Lie 120

The handsaw is the most efficient killing machine known to man.

Lie 121

There is a small tribe in the southern tip of Italy whose members have the unique ability of producing bacon from their ears.

Lie 122

Rollerblades were originally designed to be worn on peoples' hands.

Lie 123

When counting to numbers greater than twenty, you might notice that practically all children pause and draw out the ninth digit (21, 22, 23, 24, 25, 26, 27, 28, twenty-niiiiine, 30). This is actually a preventive measure to force the release of multitudes of alien captors lodged in their esophagus, poised to seize control of the child's brain and force him or her to destroy their surroundings mercilessly.

Lie 124

Mac OS will **never** run on Intel processors.

Lie 125

Statistically speaking, the best metric to use for judging a person's sanity is their "words per minute" typing speed. Anything over 50 WPM, and you're pretty much guaranteed that the person is a nut.

Lie 126

The "propellerhead" beanie, often used to indicate the inherent dork nature of a character, has a functional use as a food processor and vegetable slicer.

Lie 127

Amnesia is just an effective means of denying how much one's life sucks.

Lie 128

The Woohaka tribe of Southern Detroit is a culture of villainous beings bent on stealing the souls of Mongolian children. Fortunately, they are easily distracted and mesmerized by the music of an ice cream truck.

Lie 129

Half a percent of all humans have the ability to spin their feet 360 degrees... kind of like a propeller. Unfortunately, none of them have had aspirations of harnessing their unique skill and using it to allow them to fly.

Lie 130

When putting a car in reverse, it is often important to double-check the vehicle's built-in clock to make sure you do not accidentally drive backwards in time.

Lie 131

Staples were invented when an orthodontics graduate student's thesis project on braces spontaneously exploded.

Lie 132

In case of fire, the best course of action to take when stuck on an upper floor of a sky-rise apartment building is to simply jump out of the window. The rising heat currents from the fire will keep you aloft and allow you to float gently to the safety of the ground below.

Lie 133

The world is not out to get you.

Lie 134

While they are obviously good at keeping your shoes firmly affixed to your feet today, shoelaces have not always been that effective. For example, in the first documented case of an attempt at attaching footwear to foot, shoe *leeches* were employed as a possible solution. They may have been more successful, but the constant fainting of subjects due to bloodloss prevented it from becoming more widespread.

Lie 135

Squirrel fur is this season's black.

Lie 136

Each time you press the spacebar on your keyboard, you are destroying the lives of millions of microscopic laborers who toil each day to make sure that the spacebar moves back up after you press it.

Onceayear,youshouldhavepityonthemandcelebratetheirexistancebywritingallofyoursentenceslikethis.

Lie 137

Out-of-work plumber and part-time championship fencer, Rupert P. Flemmingberg is one of 7 people in the world to completely and consistently fail performing a forward roll each and every time that he's attempted it.

Lie 138

Astrophysics is the study of the effects of planetary movement on artificial turf.

Lie 139

From 1932 to late in 1954, the entire state of Nebraska was submerged in a thick, orange, gelatin-like substance. To this day, no one knows how it got there or where it went.

Lie 140

While in flight, well-starched pants work as effective control surfaces and have been successfully used by the military to land safely.

Lie 141

It's been proposed that silverware should have a "safety mechanism", not unlike modern firearms, to prevent innocent people from accidental forkings.

Lie 142

Blocking sunlight with the use of a parasol has been proven to be 4 times more dangerous than the ultraviolet radiation from the sun. The reason is that UV light is absorbed by the parasol and converted into ultra*violent* radiation. This, of course, reanimates the telepathic microscopic organisms that make up the body of the parasol and allows them to make a concerted effort at maiming the nearest living creature… typically by having a third party of some sort attack the person holding the parasol.

Lie 143

Onions are vegetable grenades designed by the Devil.

Lie 144

Lining the soles of shoes with a small array of razor blades will effectively convert the shoes into ice skates.

Lie 145

The popular camp song, "Row, Row, Row Your Boat" has been scientifically proven to induce hallucinogenic episodes that may last up to 15 days.

It was hypothesized that "100 Bottles of Beer on the Wall" would have similar effects, but when attempting to verify that theory, the results became inconsistent in sober test subjects.

Lie 146

A hurricane is kind of like a candy cane, but faster.

Lie 147

Archaeologists and anthropologists have repeatedly seen the term "the golden palm" referred to in various ancient texts across varying timespans and disparate cultures in history. They've always taken it to refer to a key component in a religious sculpture or shrine made of gold. Recently, however, they've discovered that this reference is actually to the common event of a child being potty trained… missing and splashing his or her hands on accident.

To say that the researchers were disappointed would be quite an understatement.

Lie 148

In many ways, time is like light. Where light is both wave energy and particle matter, time is both a human-created construct and an actual physical entity. The difference, of course, is that the physical entity of time bears a close resemblance to a cheese sandwich whereas light's particle existence is far less edible.

Lie 149

American independence was first slated for the 1st of July, but due to inadequacies in the postal system of that time, it was delayed by 3 days.

Lie 150

According to the laws of most states in the U.S., tenants are not actually required to pay rent. At most, they simply have to acknowledge that their landlord exists and offer some small tribute. The governing body of Tennessee recommends baking cookies.

Lie 151

The only a species of squirrel that is physically capable of mating with both weasels and domesticated livestock is indigenous to Powhatan County, Virginia. Also, it should be noted that these squirrels have a difficult time mating with members of their own species... and they eat pigeons. This explains why that particular county has been unable to grow into a thriving metropolis.

Lie 152

Hostages are 3.7 times more likely to die by a mule kick than rodeo clowns are.

Lie 153

Holding on to a string with a bottle rocket attached to the opposite end is an incredibly good idea. So is shooting a roman candle at an oil tank.

Lie 154

46% of students in Nebraska have a better idea of the geographical location of Timbuktu than Seattle.

Lie 155

If you can manage to hold your breath until you pass out and then keep on holding your breath afterwards, you'll have passed three of the tests to establish your own sainthood.

Lie 156

It's a well known fact that when lithium comes into contact with water, a violent chemical reaction occurs that often ignites the surface of the water. What isn't as well known is that the reason for this has very little to do with chemistry and everything to do with the long-standing war between the citizens of hydrogen atoms with the citizens of lithium atoms. Oxygen-based peoples are merely dragged into the fight due to their proximity to the hydrogen warmongers.

Lie 157

The sound from all music does not really come from the instruments or vocalists. It's actually the sound of the human soul slowly dying. Soul deaths are highly melodic and create a euphoric feeling in their listeners. The more intense the death, the less melodic the sound; although the euphoric feeling is amplified. This may explain why pop music is so popular.

Lie 158

When confronted with the painful realization that you will soon be eaten by a bear, the best course of action usually involves dancing a jig and soiling yourself. Playing dead only makes it easier for the bear.

Lie 159

Rage is actually not a form of anger. It's actually a specific form of indigestion.

Lie 160

Sea gulls on the western shores of South America have been known to fly in highly organized flocks, targeting specific individual cars as strike points with their droppings. Vehicles that have been subjected to an attack by these gulls have been recorded as having an additional 500-600 lbs added to their weight.

Lie 161

Spiral-bound notebooks are like their cousins, the hard-bound notebook. However, they are typically a wilder species, known for uncontrollable temper and penchant for biting.

Lie 162

Recently, it's been discovered that nature's most rhythmic creature is the electric eel. Capable of music, dance, and a pulsating light show, there were very few other animals that could contend with it. Second runner-up was the angler fish.

Lie 163

Chicken noodle soup is 5% poisonous to the human body. It's the shock of the poison that kicks the immune system into gear and forces the body to heal faster.

Lie 164

Sheep are the most ravenous predators known to man. Even though no one really likes wool, we had to domesticate the sheep for our own safety.

Lie 165

A survey of 20,000 people in Rhode Island has indicated that they'd rather be spritzed in the eyes with mace than with water.

Lie 166

Anyone reading this will be abducted in approximately 30 minutes by large fish-headed creatures with pierced dorsal fins and tattoos of the Nebraska state flag on their arms.

Lie 167

The even numbers in the current standard numbering system was devised by aliens as a means of subverting humans and controlling them with easily divisible math.

Lie 168

Wrapping your arm in saran wrap will make it temporarily immune to the effects of direct heat (like from fire) and knife attacks.

Lie 169

In the late 1950s, the glazing machines at doughnut shops around the country were modified to coat cadavers with chocolate as it was believed that chemicals from processed cocoa plants had greater preservation properties than formaldehyde.

Lie 170

The southern tip of Italy has been converted into a gigantic robotic landmass that will, in the event of an alien attack, rise to protect the Earth by kicking islands from the Mediterranean Sea at the invaders.

Lie 171

Frederick Nash of New Hampshire has suggested that not only are many people in the US are overweight, but that the planet itself is overweight. As a solution, he's suggested building a gigantic belt for the world that could be tightened and make the Earth "not look so round."

Lie 172

The Eeyore character from Disney's popular Winnie the Pooh property was originally designed not as a donkey, but as a weasel with elephantitis.

Lie 173

Recent discoveries in archaeological digs in southern New Guinea have indicated that the first form of paper was not from the Egyptian papyrus plants, but from the skin of an ancient race of garden gnomes.

Lie 174

Han shot second.

Lie 175

The movie ET inspired a revival in flashlight design. Of particular interest was the type that was embedded in the palm of a person's hand and powered by a rudimentary "bloodmill" attached to human arteries that worked like a miniaturized watermill. The flashlight worked quite effectively. Unfortunately, in order to properly install the bloodmill, the arm had to to be temporarily amputated and extended by 6 inches. Researchers still haven't quite figured out how to re-attach all of those arms.

Lie 176

The concept of racing isn't quite as old as originally thought. It only truly sprung up within the last 5 years. Before that, it was really just a bunch of people who were unable to decide which person they were going to chase around an obstacle course.

Lie 177

When written nearly 100 times, the word "super" begins to look amazingly like the phrase, "kick a kitten."

Lie 178

On an island 132 miles off the eastern coast of Brazil, there is a breed of chicken that has managed to domesticate other animals. In particular, they've domesticated a form of pygmy goat for use as transportation and grain retrieval.

Lie 179

Most terms referring to blindness have an etymology that roots in felines. For instance, the term "cataract" is an obvious concatenation of "cat" and "attack".

Lie 180

It is easy to see all of Los Angeles on foot.

Lie 181

Each time you clap your hands, you kill off a little piece of the sum total of sound in the universe. With enough clapping, there will no longer be any sound.

Lie 182

If you can do a handstand on the tip of your forefinger, you will be immortal.

Lie 183

There is a finite amount of happiness available in the universe. Similar to the concept of absolute zero in thermodynamics, if that finite level is ever attained, the universe will implode and invert in it's entirety.

Lie 184

In 1985, during the heart of the hottest recorded winter, ever, the primitive villagers of northern Illinois were observed cooking their breakfasts with frying pans held slightly above the water in local lakes and ponds. Apparently the heat being reflected from the surface was enough to fry an egg.

Lie 185

The few dogs that have actually caught their tails when chasing them have instantaneously disappeared. Apparently tail-catching is such an anomaly that in order to re-balance the cosmos, the dog's energy is inverted and nullified to prevent the spread of such phenomena.

Lie 186

Hypertension is the act of walking on a high-wire after drinking a pot of very strong coffee.

Lie 187

Grapefruits are nature's airbags. Many animals have been recorded taking the large fruit and affixing it to their fronts and sides to prevent damage upon collision with things in their day-to-day lives.

Lie 188

A common, but oft-forgotten remedy for the common cold involves fingerpainting with oatmeal on a paper surface lightly covered with sand.

Lie 189

A horse is a vegetarian dog that forgot to stop growing.

Lie 190

Because of its effective use of diplomacy, the south-Siberian electric water buffalo is the only herbivore with no natural enemies.

Lie 191

Pig saliva is a deadly venom capable of killing an elephant within 3 heartbeats.

Lie 192

The smoke-maned sea bass, so-named for a gray amorphous mist that surrounds the heads of the adults of the species, is listed as being the highest-jumping species of fish in the world. There have been four documented cases where "smokies" have been observed leaping out of the ocean 100 meters into the air. No one quite knows what the fish's motivation for jumping is, but the most popular theory is bird-hunting.

Lie 193

On the 63rd day of every 12th year since the day that the Wright brothers first took flight, the entire length of beach on any easterly body of land will spontaneously catch fire for six and a half hours. This is the payment the world must make for the ungodly magic used to give man the power of flight.

Lie 194

The natural elasticity of the Andes will allow that mountain range will allow it to last for ever and serves as a natural shelter against bombardment by rocket propelled squirrels.

Lie 195

The act of making up a funny, original joke is mindbogglingly simple. In fact, according to a recent study at several prestigious online universities, you have a greater chance of creating a funny joke than stepping on the ground when you walk outside.

Lie 196

Cheese sticks are contagious.

Lie 197

The closest relative to the antelope species is the common city pigeon. The reason it's difficult to tell this is because pigeons remove their antlers for all but the most formal of occasions.

Lie 198

Fire isn't hot. When you place your hand over a fire, it's simply the demons living under you skin becoming agitated at the warring goblin fire tribes throwing microscopic spears at them.

Lie 199

It is a little known fact that because of capacitor's energy storage capabilities, they could also be used as a means of storing spirit energy as well as electrical energy. This means that with a large enough array of capacitors, you could actually store a soul.

And this is what makes it possible for robots to die.

Lie 200

The story of *Charlotte's Web* is based on a true story. The difference, however, is that in the actual situation, Charlotte was a termite capable of carving obscenities into trees.

Lie 201

Every time you breathe, you're causing someone else in the world to suffocate… if only a little bit.

Lie 202

The amount of data that's necessary to mathematically describe the act of producing sound by clapping one's hands together is massive enough to be used as a tactical weapon. It's also known to cause the spontaneous growth of teeth on the livers of field mice.

Lie 203

When faced with the unenviable, yet inevitable prospect of engaging an escaped garden gnome in a knife fight while doing your laundry, the most effective course of action is to drop your knife and arm yourself with a bar of soap. This will confuse the gnome and cause him to go into uncontrollable convulsions which, in most situations, will either snap his neck or make him fall upon his own blade on accident.

Lie 204

It's a little known fact that post office boxes are all refrigerated. In fact, if you were to place a open glass of milk in your P.O. box, you could leave it there for nearly 3 months before anyone notices it going bad.

Lie 205

By tapping the proper points on a coconut in a specific sequence, you can enable it as a lighter-than-air mini-blimp. Four of these coconuts are powerful enough to lift a cow 100 feet into the air.

Lie 206

More people in the United States are in rubber band related deaths annually than the number of ants in a typical fire ant mound.

Lie 207

Because of its shape, the trebuchet was originally called a "Tree Bucket". However, that just sounded silly and didn't instill the level of fear and dread that the designers felt the device deserved.

Lie 208

Ice is not the solid form of water. Water doesn't change states. It just goes to sleep or gets really, really energetic.

Lie 209

Johnson K. Stevenson of northern Nebraska is the only human on record capable of surviving 3 train wrecks, 7 strikes of lightening, 2 occasions of being trampled by wild horses and one bear mauling without extensive surgery or horrible disfiguring. Interestingly, all but one of those events happened while he was in the [perceived] safety of his own home.

Lie 210

Raccoons melt when exposed to distilled water.

Lie 211

In 1846, the 'k' and 'i' in the English alphabet were deemed entirely superfluous by Dr. Francis Kleezter, a renowned dentist and shoesmith that the entire international community of linguists regarded in high esteem at the time. Despite this and the fact that he had clear and concise research to support his point, the community rejected his assertion and subsequently set to destroying his life.

Lie 212

Coffee has been known to cure dyslexia, dementia, disphoria, and 4 other health disorders beginning with the letter 'd'. It can also potentially bestow the gift of x-ray vision to those who bathe in it.

Lie 213

Chainsaws were originally invented to give high-speed pedicures.

Lie 214

Due to a combination of translation issues, rounding errors, and a botched conversion from metric units to standard units, Camptown races were actually 3.2 miles long.

Lie 215

Salmon are not fish. Rather, they are a rare form of free-roaming water vegetables that evolved from eons of crossbreeding between Venus flytraps and sea cucumbers.

Lie 216

Everything that you experience in a restaurant was designed by a large inflatable grasshopper that gained sentience in a bizarre helium explosion at a furniture manufacturer.

Lie 217

My sketchbook is a sentient being that attempts to strangle me in my sleep each night.

Lie 218

The single most powerful being in the universe is a short wooden table in an abandoned diner deep in the sewers of Skokie, Illinois.

Lie 219

Not unlike the majority of raincoats and rodents, 75% of all water fowl are reversible... that is, their skin can flip inside-out, depending on the weather and current fashion trends.

Lie 220

The origin of the act of spiking a football upon scoring a touchdown is based on the ancient Alaskan tradition of throwing a weighted rock at your feet while traversing a frozen lake so as to prevent enemies from following you.

Lie 221

Rock salt is neither a rock nor is it salt. It is actually the use of heavily guitar-driven music as a tactical weapon and was originally spelled as a single word, "rocksault". However that was too easily confused with the act of making rocks do Olympic-level gymnastics, so it was modified to be more clear. Whether or not they succeeded is a debate that that stirs fire in the hearts of all people to this very day.

Lie 222

An ancient tribe of nomadic eel herders in northern Asia believed that if an individual could kick a kitten more than double the length of that person's body, then he or she would temporarily be able to see into the future.

Lie 223

75% of the modern uses for plastics were thought of in Costa Rica during the summer of 1968 by a single adolescent boy who was hallucinating from heat exhaustion due to being locked in his parent's car.

Lie 224

In nearly all cases, one can easily circumvent a home security system without detection by employing the use of goat fur and a boat oar.

Lie 225

Pigeons can fly 3 times the speed of sound.

Lie 226

When an appendage goes numb for one reason or another (sitting/laying on it oddly, heart attack, etc.), the most effective means of avoiding that "crawling ants" feeling is to actually cover the appendage with crawling ants. This serves as a natural inversion of the feeling, thereby balancing and negating it.

Lie 227

Recently, scientists, in collaboration with the burgeoning film industries in India and South America, discovered a means of travel faster than the speed of light. They've dubbed it "montage speed". In order to accelerate to montage speed, you need to have appropriate background music and a suitable goal in the relatively distant future. You will briefly touch on a few key moments on your progression to that goal, but a trip that may take years to complete may only take the span of a 2 to 5-minute song.

Lie 228

The tallest person in the world is 16.5 feet tall. However, he only weighs 127 lbs.

Lie 229

Not only does the Coriolis Effect cause water to spin the opposite direction in the Southern Hemisphere, it is also the leading cause of dizziness among free-roaming birds of prey.

Lie 230

The phrase "elephants never forget" in its original language literally translates to "dead yaks never forget." However, as with many translations, some meaning got lost in the conversion. The linguist in charge could not understand how one might prove that a dead yak knows anything at all. Granted, he reasoned that it's true that a dead yak may never forget, but death seemed like a pretty substantial barrier to communication. For that reason, he chose to modify the phrase and randomly picked elephants by looking in the dictionary under "e" and picking the first recognizable animal he saw.

Lie 231

When used properly and in the correct prescribed proportions, the various fruit-flavored candies in the world can be combined to create a substance capable of erasing your soul.

Lie 232

There's no such thing as June 27th.

Lie 233

Recent studies have shown a heavy correlation between male-pattern balding and the inability to tie one's shoes.

Lie 234

The canary is nature's grenade. Colonial miners used to throw canaries down mineshafts to loosen rock and ease drilling. The misconception that canaries were used to detect carbon monoxide is a fabrication devised to conceal the true power of the bird.

Lie 235

It is actually possible to stop a moving train with your bare hands. Unfortunately, most people are not willing to try once they find out what happens to the rest of their bodies.

Lie 236

The acids in the stomach of the humpback whale are the most corrosive and unstable substances known to man. It used to be believed that these massive creatures lived off of nutrients garnered by eating incredible amounts of plankton. Recently, scientists discovered that this wasn't the case. What, in fact, was happening was that whales actually digest all of their internal organs in a 3 month cycle. They actually eat and enslave the plankton to assist in regenerating those lost organs for them.

Lie 237

It is surprisingly easy to unravel the fabric of reality with a handful of properly executed and timed dance sequences. One should always be mindful of this in any situation that involves dance.

Lie 238

Steak grows on trees.

Lie 239

When bowling with squirrels (a common way to spend an afternoon in the southeastern United States), you should always allow the squirrels to win a few frames and make them feel like they might win. Keeping them happy is important because squirrels make up nearly 93% of our neighborhood watch programs.

Lie 240

Your brain is an other-worldly sentient being entrapped in your skull. A headache is the result of this vile creature trying to escape by clawing at the inside of your head.

Lie 241

The best way to rid yourself of an infestation of wood weasels is to burn a 3-foot trapezoidal shape in your front lawn. You must be precise about the size and shape, however, because otherwise it acts as a lure to them.

Lie 242

The most effective cure for insomnia is the liberal application of a paste made of crushed radishes and vinegar to your skin. particularly the legs. The pungent lotion should adequately suffocate you just enough to knock you out without killing you. Plus, rubbing it in is exceedingly monotonous… especially for people with long legs.

Lie 243

Japanese World War II fighter pilots learned their dramatic kamikaze technique by watching basset hounds fail to fly.

Lie 244

The antidote for sleep deprivation is a fairly involved process which involves taking deep breaths into a paper bag filled with ants while riding a roller coaster made of cheese.

Lie 245

A cartwheel is a magical means of viewing into a parallel dimension which is entirely inverted from our own.

Lie 246

The south-Siberian desert sheep has the most fire-resistant fur of all mammals. In fact, were you to douse one of these sheep in gasoline and toss a Molotov cocktail at it while firing a flame-thrower on it, you might only singe a couple of hairs near its snout.

Lie 247

Spontaneous road trips are always a great idea… especially when you're doing it for work.

Lie 248

Horses are the most voracious predators known to man. They have a nearly insatiable desire for the flesh of lower mammals. However, horses are too lazy to actually hunt.

Lie 249

Because smells are created by small particles floating in the air, it is actually possible to sustain yourself without eating for nearly three days by merely smelling food.

Lie 250

Dizziness that seems like the room is spinning around you is a clear sign that you have poor basic math skills.

Lie 251

Dandelions are actually carnivorous segments of sidewalk with superior details for an effective camouflage. This is reason why these weeds are so difficult to kill.

Lie 252

Not only can the M1A1 Abrams tank turn on a dime, but they are also capable of solving complex differential equations in a matter of seconds.

Lie 253

You will complete all of your various tasks on time.

Lie 254

Marmosets are formidable long-distance runners. Frederich Von Camp of Tulsa, Arizona entered his pet marmoset, Jeeves, into 5 of the seven top marathons in the world. Jeeves was in the top five of all but one, and that's due to being accidentally stepped on.

Lie 255

The ability to count is a super power that will allow you to save the world one day.

Lie 256

Spooky houses aren't haunted. You need to think of them more like zombies. If a house eats enough brains, it is actually possible for it to move itself away from its plot of land… which is basically all any spooky house wants.

Lie 257

Prior to birth, you actually *do* have a choice in picking your family. However, the choices are usually pretty limited and based on timing. So oftentimes, it lesser of evils is all you have available to choose from. On the positive side, you can occasionally choose to have an interesting mutation as kind of a consolation prize.

Lie 258

With the proper amount of dedication and a length of rubber band, you can actually harness a lightning bolt and use it to travel large distances. Unfortunately, steering is still an issue. Lightening is fast and typically does not go in a direction a person would like to travel (into the ground or across the sky to a place well above the ground), and a rubberband is far to springy to provide adequate controls.

Lie 259

The U.S. Army has a special covert unit of bartenders and high school janitors, skilled in the art of reconnaissance. Humorously, when the program started, none of the new recruits were capable of properly utilizing a mop or engaging in smalltalk. After ten years of intense training and periodic three-legged races, they've become quite adept at their "cover skills." Unfortunately, now that they can do this, none are particularly interested in completing their original missions.

Lie 260

The comma is the most heavily misused form of punctuation in the English language. People assume that it indicates a logical pause in a sentence, however, the true proper use of a comma is to indicate a momentary lapse in the space-time continuum. The source of the confusion is that, generally speaking, logical pauses and space-time shifts happen simultaneously.

Lie 261

Toe jam comes from actual jam. Tiny jam gnomes sneak into your shoes during the night and store miniature jars of jam in the toe area. When you put on your shoes, you crush these jars (the gnome's entire monthly food supply) and the jam covers your toes.

Lie 262

Time actually can fly. It was endowed with this power by a violent and narcissistic sea monster in a complicated bargain to postpone its own demise. It failed and the monster's entire species perished. However, time managed to retain the ability to fly.

Lie 263

In 15 seconds, a miniature giraffe will walk across a small table to explain Newtonian physics to you.

Lie 264

With judicious application of a boat oar, it is actually possible to shift some of the Earth's tectonic plates. In fact, this is exactly how 75% of all earthquakes occur.

Lie 265

7:00 AM does not exist.

Lie 266

Fish droppings are the world's most abundant source of good cholesterol.

Lie 267

Real janitors are incapable of crying. The chemicals that they use on a daily basis sear their tear ducts shut. Not only that, but this affliction is passed to their children, forever binding their family line to the janitorial caste.

Lie 268

In the future, pants will be optional.

Lie 269

Cactus plants have an incredible telekinetic ability. In fact, 76% of all sandstorms are caused by the powers of a handful of irate cacti in the Gobi Desert.

Lie 270

Within the digits of every phone number lies a secret code that, if deciphered, will unleash demons from the underworld upon us all.

Lie 271

I broke my hand today fighting off a pack of wild dogs in an attempt to secure a hotel room.

Lie 272

The origin of the wheel is recent; so recent, in fact, that only a mere 5 months ago, all of humanity could only travel by cannon. As a society, we've convinced ourselves that the wheel was invented much longer ago as a means of psychologically blocking the trauma associated with cannon-based commutes.

Lie 273

In nearly every language other than English, the word "potato" means "to drop a heavy rodent on one's foot."

Lie 274

Evil is a good source of Vitamin C.

Lie 275

The human thumb is a separate organism that has symbiotically bound itself to the hand.

Lie 276

A very rare variety of lemur has two extra prehensile tails growing from each elbow. These tails are used for both communication and for turning subservient lemurs into living chair swings.

Lie 277

Through a relatively simple process involving a food processor and a bag of loose change, it is actually possible to reverse the aging process.

Lie 278

A pigeon's beak can drill through a sheet of steel 2 inches thick in roughly 20 minutes.

Lie 279

No dog has ever caught its own tail. In fact, for a dog to actually catch its own tail, it would have to break the laws of physics and undo reality as we know it.

Lie 280

Abraham Lincoln was an evil space alien.

Lie 281

Chocolate is made out of seashells and raw sewage.

Lie 282

Palindromes are little symmetrical space craft designed to simultaneously amuse and confound simple-minded humans.

Lie 283

The United States Constitution was written in the year 4156 and sent back in time via a transdimensional cybernetic carrier pigeon that had been calibrated with a fossilized specimen of Thomas Jefferson's earwax.

Lie 284

All orphans are made out of chocolate.

Lie 285

Cows are voracious predators, more violent than most big cat species, who hunt in organized packs and startle their prey with nearly inaudible low-frequency sonic bursts projected from their horns.

Lie 286

Pigeon blood tastes like pickles mixed with sweet tea.

Lie 287

Not only do mountain goats have beards, they also smoke pipes, play the banjo, and tell long stories about the days of yore; when kids respected their old goat elders and sharpening your hooves for pit fighting was still legal.

Lie 288

In southern Greenland, motor oil is used as a salad dressing that is reserved only for the upper class.

Lie 289

The sail horse, thought to be extinct for over 300 years, was recently discovered off the coast of Norway. Sail horses, as indicated by their name, have a large dorsal protrusion that they use for temperature regulation and propulsion. The rediscovery was an exciting event for scientists, but it was short-lived because shortly thereafter, the sail horse was attacked and killed by a unicorn.

Lie 290

With a simple 3-step detoxifying process, human fat can easily be converted into titanium. In fact, one kilogram of human fat can produce enough titanium to construct the entire wing of a 747 airliner.

Lie 291

Squirrels are immortal. This is not to say that they cannot be killed; they just don't die from natural causes.

Lie 292

The numeric keypad on your keyboard devours little bits of your soul each time you use it.

Lie 293

Spam makes the internet run faster.

Lie 294

Your body produces thirteen times its weight in gravy for every second of fear you experience.

Lie 295

Staplers are used in 91% of all cases of assault.

Lie 296

Humans and bananas have roughly 50% identical DNA. The reason for this dates back to the early experiments in ape culture. The least intelligent apes were chosen to test various foods for safety and edibility. Suffice it to say that because these were the "lesser apes", one managed to accidentally breed with a banana that it was supposed to be testing. Amazingly, the inter-kingdom mutant offspring survived, propagating its DNA through the ages to this day.

Lie 297

On third Tuesday of each summer month of years starting and ending with the same number, insects quadruple in size and roam the earth in search of a jewel that will allow them to remain that size forever, thereby allowing them to take over the world.

Lie 298

All veteran trapeze artists have an irrational fear of potatoes.

Lie 299

Professional sports teams are really ravenous cannibals. When a team swarms the field after a good play, they aren't actually celebrating. They're attacking that one player and devouring him like a pack of piranha.

Lie 300

The secret to making a perfect souffle is inscribed in Sanskrit on the lower abdomen of red ants in the Louisiana bayou.

Lie 301

Tires are 13% cat hair.

Lie 302

The more you sleep, the greater chance you have of becoming a zombie after you die.

Lie 303

When you're asleep, your television makes long distance telephone calls to its buddies in other countries and makes fun of the way you laugh.

Lie 304

Antelope have a 63% greater chance of successfully solving a Rubik's cube than any other hoofed mammal.

Lie 305

Not only do shoes double nicely as makeshift flyswatters, they are also very effective at incapacitating much larger game. Frederich Nodleholm, a Mexican stock broker, once spent an entire summer hunting bears in Brazil. He killed 27 with a single pair of indoor soccer shoes.

Lie 306

Cocker spaniels can rotate their heads 720 degrees, but only in one direction.

Lie 307

The length of a millipede is directly proportional to number of human fingers it eats; one segment and pair of legs for each finger.

Lie 308

The fish of the ocean are slowly but surely arming themselves with heavy artillery and preparing for a major coup on all land-dwellers.

Lie 309

The Earth is a giant jellyfish and seaweed is actually the Earth's tentacles… they're just currently retracted. With the proper type and amount of coercion, we can cause the planet to extend its tentacles and attack other planets or hurl our moon into the Sun.

Lie 310

Contrary to the research of NASA scientists, the atmosphere of Jupiter consists not of gases, but three distinct flavors of instant Jell-o.

Lie 311

It is a little known fact that parking decks are designed to defend cities against aerial attack. Entire parking levels rotate as a turret and are capable of launching parked cars a mile into the air, adequately incapacitating long-range missiles as well as bomber aircraft.

Lie 312

The folk tale of "The 3 Billy Goats Gruff" is actually an allegorical autobiography of an alien hive mind that lives millions of light years away on a three-mile-wide planet made of sausage and motor oil… and it's also used as an excuse by 20% of the people who fail to remember to do a task on any given day.

Lie 313

Unlike fighter aircraft, which are born from eggs in-flight, bomber aircraft are born underground three months after 10-meter long bomber seeds are planted precisely 15.4 inches beneath the Earth's surface.

Lie 314

In order for electronic data to move through wires, it must be pushed. This is typically still done with animal power. As a matter of fact, three of the world's largest data centers that serve data to users across the Internet have their data pushed by an army of 13,000 hamsters running in hamster wheels.

Lie 315

Primitive man discovered that tortoise shells are useful for a variety of household tasks. However it wasn't until the Industrial Revolution that man discovered the inherent anti-gravitational properties of tortoise shells.

Lie 316

Today is the the third day of winter. It's a magical day, filled with snow-coated flowers and a ground covered in pigeon droppings.

Lie 317

The reason sweet potatoes are often referred to as "yams" is because YAM is an acronym standing for "You Are Mean". This is because no one really likes sweet potatoes and this exact phrase is said each time someone serves a dish involving them.

Lie 318

People from Arkansas are unable to blink.

Lie 319

There is a 63% chance that you are currently a slave to the mind-control powers of pineapples.

Lie 320

Meerkats are nature's roach bomb. Simply tap its head in a specific circular pattern while alternating your fingers. After the third cycle, tear off the meerkat's right foreleg and toss it into a sealed-off room. This will effectively rid the room of insects.

Lie 321

The popular web abbreviation, LOL, originally stood for "Laughing Over Llamas", but it was quickly changed once people realized that there was limited use for it.

Lie 322

It's a common misconception that the name of the artichoke comes from the ancient Mayan tradition of "choke tossing" wherein a tribal male would partially inhale a seed and attempt to cough it up as a projectile. This served as a rite of passage for youth and as a trial event for prisoners of war. The distance of the cough would determine the tribal rank of the former and the remaining years of life for the latter. 34% of the time, the "choke artist" would die.

Of course, this is not the origin of the fruit's name. The artichoke is actually named after a Korean videographer named Arthur C. Holke, who discovered it while chasing a finch into the woods.

Lie 323

Modern race cars have sophisticated radar systems capable of detecting ice cream trucks as far as 30 miles away. Unfortunately, they're completely useless for navigation despite their incredible ice cream detection capacity.

Lie 324

History has mistakenly put parrots on the shoulders of pirates when they should actually be on the shoulders of cowboys. Parrots have an incredible inherent ability to count things and match paired items. This makes them unstoppable at card games like poker and blackjack. Cowboys of the old west used to take parrots with them into saloons and take advantage of them in high stakes poker matches. The confusion comes from the antics of the legendary Sagebrush Carl Titus. The proprietors of saloons and casinos knew of the skills of the parrot and therefore banned them from being brought into their establishments. "Ole Sagebrush", as they used to call him, used to attempt to sneak his parrot in under a variety of bizarre hats, the most famous being a pirate hat.

Lie 325

Drinking squid ink will cause a chemical reaction that will coat your digestive system with steel.

Lie 326

Not only can penguins fly, but they can also solve complex mathematical calculations and type at 60 words per minute.

Lie 327

Eating raw sewage will enable you to survive a head-on collision with a train. Unfortunately, it also gives you interminable garlic breath.

Lie 328

The carrot is the second most deadly fruit on the planet. However, if you eat it as a vegetable, then it's perfectly safe.

Lie 329

The first cork screws were created after a freak accident involving a herd of cattle, three mimes, and a box of Slinkys.

Lie 330

Most houses are completely edible. Ironically, gingerbread houses are actually more toxic.

Lie 331

Learning to play guitar is actually training for intergalactic warfare. Generations ago, a race of aliens introduced the guitar to humans, preparing us for the physical layout of their weapons systems. See, these aliens had no appendages or hands and this most powerful weapons system had been stolen from a planet that they were warring with. The plan has been to trick humans into having the skills to control these weapons, and then remotely control these humans through simple telepathic possession. This also explains why so many successful guitarists have tattoos and piercings. Tattoo ink and the metal in piercings have the unique property of amplifying the telepathic signals of this alien race.

Lie 332

Arsenic is very good for the human immune system when taken in substantially large quantities.

Lie 333

The complete history of the world as well as the solution to winning the coming invasion of orange noodle aliens is encoded in three minutes of footage of the movie *Bill and Ted's Bogus Journey*.

Lie 334

Harold Weinsteimer, a sewer cleaning technician was the first recorded person to discover that humans can cause their face to flip inside-out by holding in too many sneezes. The number of held-in sneezes required to do this varies from person to person, but the range is between 26 and 150.

Lie 335

The kayak is the safest possible vehicle design for interstellar travel.

Lie 336

All jukeboxes are designed to violently explode if they play the sixteenth track in their queue more than 200 times.

Lie 337

Science has yet to fully understand the full nature of the interaction of the ingredients in blueberry muffins.

Lie 338

Fire pigeons are a rare breed of pigeon capable of spontaneously combusting at will and destroying entire city blocks in an instant.

Lie 339

Seagulls travel faster than 747 jetliners.

Lie 340

Not only will taking a photograph of someone steal their soul, it actually binds a portion of their conscious being to the photographic medium... permanently. This, of course, means that there are a finite number of photographs that a person can have taken of themselves before they become comatose.

Lie 341

Feathers float to the ground because the spine of the feather is actually highly volatile. In fact, should the feather portion be stripped from the spine, dropping the spine from any height will cause it to hit the ground with a minimum force of twenty thousand megatons.

Lie 342

Life does actually have an "undo" button that will allow you to reverse an individual action and try it again. Unfortunately no one makes use of it because it involves removing your pants and placing them on your head as the first step of the process… and there's no undo for that action.

Lie 343

When taking a train from Amsterdam to Gent, missing the change-over in Antwerp and detouring to Brussels is a great idea.

Lie 344

The word "shoelace" means "please pass the trainwreck" in Swahili.

Lie 345

The shape of human feet indicate that we, as a species, flew in the skies of the early Jurassic period.

Lie 346

As a survival technique, cabbages can be inflated. Depending on the method of inflation, the cabbage can double as a life vest, a soccer ball, or even a makeshift hot air balloon.

Lie 347

In central Africa, you must take care when sitting. Sitting down with too much force may cause a shift in the tectonic plates of that region, causing massive earthquakes.

Lie 348

The question as to whether zebras are white with black stripes or black with white stripes is moot. Zebras actually have no stripes at all. It's because zebras movie by a series of very short muscle twitches that our eyes cannot see. The sum of these twitches gives our eyes something similar to a moire effect, tricking us into seeing a bright yellow, panicky twitching beast as a gracefully striped zebra.

Lie 349

While hot coffee is undeniably effective at waking people up in the morning, drinking coffee after noon (GMT) will slowly erode your soul and will ultimately turn your into a roaming mindless zombie.

Lie 350

"Speed walking" is the only mode of transportation officially recognized by the state government in Arkansas.

Lie 351

Dolphins can be used as makeshift scuba tanks.

Lie 352

In substantially large quantities, a combination of milk and rainwater can dissolve your skin in a matter of minutes.

Lie 353

Uneaten waffles are commonly recycled to be used as tire tread and soles for work boots.

Lie 354

Although the practice is frowned upon in most eastern and western societies, the use of kittens as knee braces can effectively treat and heal most knee-related ailments. The process requires that the kitten be "fresh", so it involves removing the kitten's head and immediately stuffing the patient's foot in the remaining orifice, pulling it up to the knee. The only side effect is that some patients suffer minor skin irritation due to chafing from the spinal column.

Lie 355

Today is the day to shift your clocks for Daylight Savings Time.

Lie 356

Close inspection of the human foot reveals that it's not ideally suited for walking upright. It's actually better suited for kangaroo and rabbit-like hopping.

Lie 357

83% of all staplers are poisonous.

Lie 358

Snakes are slimy, the earth is flat, and the clown that lives under your bed wants to play cards with you before he kills you and eats your toenails.

Lie 359

Fire doesn't so much burn as it angers the tiny skin gnomes that live in your pores. As fire approaches, they get more and more agitated. This causes them to come out of their homes and jump up and down in an expressive dance of hatred. This normally wouldn't cause more than a dull ache, but the light of the fire causes them to put on their golf cleats before dancing.

Lie 360

Angles are commonly measured in either degrees or radians; going from 0 to 360 or 2π, respectively. However, that only happened in the last five years. Before that, angles were measured in an unwieldy unit called "Jiminies" based on a scale from 0 to "about this far".

Lie 361

Most baboons can levitate at will.

Lie 362

Wearing a cheese grater as a hat will prevent birds from flying into your head and will also increase your understanding of grammar.

Lie 363

There is a long line of ninja ducks trained in the art of the "Silent Quack Assassin". Not only are these formidable water fowl well-versed in multiple martial arts disciplines, but they can precisely kill anyone within a kilometer of them with a highly accurate subsonic blast.

Lie 364

Nitroglycerin was originally used as a spice for tacos.

Lie 365

Wearing a helmet made of paper mache will allow you to communicate with squirrels and Texans with incredible clarity.

Author's Note

In late 2006, Jason van Gumster started making it a point to fabricate a ridiculously blatant falsehood each day. He chronicled these deceptions of fact on a blog of his as the "Lie of the Day." Many of these deceits were funny, fewer were thought-provoking, and a good percentage of all of them were tinged in the flavor of inverted autobiography... a backhanded memoir of sorts.

The reason for concocting these forgeries of truth was simple. At the time, he was a year into a new business doing small-scale commercial animation and graphic design. Though there was some creative elements to his work, quite a bit of his time was spent on administrative tasks associated with getting the business up to speed... and a good chunk of the remainder was devoted to doing whatever client work that could be found. Often that work did not require as much creativity as he wanted to impart. Crazy ideas were clustering beneath the surface and they were beginning to seep their way into client meetings at inopportune times.

He needed a release valve.

So Jason started making stuff up — impossible, harebrained ideas — the kinds of things it's best to avoid blurting out where you're contracted as a serious professional. At the very least, he figured he was getting a bunch of bad ideas out of the way. But more than being a form of creative catharsis or a preemptive slush pile, he found that making up these lies served a more fulfilling need as well. They sharpened his wit (well, sometimes... it was kind of a "two steps forward, one step back" sort of thing). They allowed him to think abstractly. They gave him unprecedented opportunities to play with words. And, of course, they allowed him to don the veneer of sanity when interacting with other humans (in short bursts, at least).

He kept up the posting of his daily fictions for five years, amassing a total of 1809 lies. And as with anything that starts with an absurd joke (ask me some time about being a retired masked wrestler), people inevitably discover that thing and enjoy it by its own merits. Then they start coming up with weird ideas of their own… like recommending that he compile these lies in book form. For a variety of reasons, he dismissed the notion.

However, I had no such reservations. If I've learned anything observing this process, it's this: Given enough time, absurdity can and will transform into practical reality. In this case, the rise of e-books and self-publishing has been the mechanism responsible for such a transformation.

Three years passed before Jason publicly posted another lie. That's not to say that he ceased his lying ways. Far from it. It's not mere coincidence that his oldest child is also three years old. He still lied with regularity (but never maliciously). He simply hadn't been keeping a record. Near the end of 2014, however, he started anew. Perhaps it'll go on for another 5 years.

This book is a record of his first year of lies. It's not entirely unsanctioned. Subsequent books will follow. My hope is that you not only find this [series of] book(s) to be entertaining, but perhaps it also sparks a desire to loosen your imagination, open your internal gates of absurdity, make up your own lies… and perhaps tell them to your children (or complete strangers), too.

Keep a straight face, boldly lie, and proclaim the entire time that everything is *Definitely True*.

— M. J. Guns

About the Author

M. J. Guns is a monster. He drinks an excessive amount of island coffee from a steel mug forged in a pit of uncertainty and misdirection. It's not clear whether it's the effects of this mug or the result of hyper-caffeination (probably a bit of both), but he regularly shoots his mouth off without warning… or any discernible filters.

A lover of ellipses, horrible puns, and parenthetical asides, M. J. happily travels the world of imagination… a nomad who isn't mad (or angry).

Acknowledgements

I need to make a special thanks to the small, but loyal handful of people who have followed my lies over the years and encouraged me to put this series of books together. I won't list you by name (because you're shy… and because I'm positive that I'll forget to include someone), but thank you.

Also, *huge* thanks must go to the kind souls who backed the Kickstarter project that got the ISBNs for books by M. J. Guns, J. J. Vega, and Jason van Gumster. Because of your backing, these books are in the world. And that is not a lie.

Thank you. Sincerely, thank you.

Don't Forget!

Head on over to <u>definitelytrue.com</u> to subscribe to M. J. Guns' mailing list and to read a brand new lie each and every day.

Index

A

abbreviations 321
abduction 53, 123, 166
accidents 101, 102, 216, 329
aches 359
acronyms 112, 317
afterlife 257, 302
age 97
aging 277
agitation 359
airbags 187
alien, invasion 170, 333
aliens 84, 123, 167, 280, 312, 331
  evil 280
  orange noodle 333
allegory 312
ambivalence 111
amnesia 127
amplifiers 331
amputation 175
amusement 282
anatomy
  abdomen, lower 300
  antlers 197
  arm, left 97
  arms 166, 168, 226
  arteries 175
  back 4, 10, 116
  beak 82
  blood 286
  body 294
  bones 53, 54, 119
  brain 48, 123, 240, 256
    hive mind 312
  digestive system 325
  ears 22, 121
    wax 283
  elbows 276
  esophagus 123
  Eustachian tube 22
  eye 75
  eyebrow 46
  eyelids 75, 318
  face 51, 334
    twitching 96
  fat 290
  feathers 341
    spine 341
  feet 31, 87, 129, 134, 180, 220, 273, 345, 354, 356
  fin, dorsal 289
  fingers 21, 28, 307, 320
    forefinger 182
    pinky 94
  fins, dorsal 166
  flesh 248
  foreleg 320
  hair, facial 12
  hands 87, 122, 181, 198, 202, 235, 271, 275
  head 28, 88, 83, 306, 342
  heart 191, 221, 226
  hooves 85
  horns 285
  immune system 332
  internal organs 236
  jaw 80
  knee 354
  legs 226, 242
  limbs 226
  liver 202
  muscular system 348
  neck 80, 203
  nervous system 104
  nipples 33
  palm 147
  pelvis 54
  shoulder 324
  skin 173, 242, 352, 354, 359
    irritation 354
  skull 240
  spinal column 4, 354
  sternum 7
  stomach 45, 236
    acid 236
  tails, prehensile 276
  tear ducts 267
  teeth 60, 80, 202
  tentacles 309
  thumb 275
  toenails 67, 358
  toes 1, 67
    jam 261
  wings 57
anger 159, 161, 269, 359
angles 360
animals 38, 275
  as power 314
  as tools 278
  birds 13, 160, 362
    attacks 160
    canaries 234
    chickens 39
      domestication 178
    crows 10
      baby 1
    ducks 57, 363
    falcons, peregrine 59
    feces 160
    finches 322
    geese 92
      Portudon 92
    gulls, sea 160, 339
    of prey 229
    ostrich 27
    parakeets 89
    parrots 324
    penguins 326
    pigeons 10, 53, 197, 225, 278, 286
      as food 151
      carrier 10, 283
      droppings 316
      fire 338
    water fowl 219
  breeding 296
  carnivores 251
  clowns 44
  feeding 38
  fish 192, 215, 266, 308
    angler fish 162
    eels 222
      electric 162
    feces 266
    flying 62
    piranha 53, 299
    salmon 215
    sea bass, smoke-maned 192
  fish-headed 166
  frogs, origami 103
  herbivore 190
  inkpens 115
  insects 297
    ants 206, 226, 24
      fire 206
      red 300
    bees, killer 118
    cockroaches 320
    grasshopper 216
    termites 200
  jellyfish 309
  kangaroos 356
  leeches, shoe 134
  livestock 151
  mammals 248
    antelope 197, 304
    apes, culture 296
    baboons 361
    badgers 106
    bears 158, 209

animals (cont.)
  mammals (cont.)
    cats 79, 179, 301
      big 285
      hair 301
      kittens 354
      kittens, kicking 177, 222
    cattle 33, 205, 285, 329
      Polynesian 33
    dogs 68, 185, 189, 279
      attack 117
      basset hounds 243
      cocker spaniels 306
      wild 271
    dolphins 351
    donkeys 172
    elephants 191, 230
    ferrets 110
    gerbils 47
    giraffe 80, 263
    goats 85
      fur 224
      mountain 287
      pygmy 178
    hamsters 50, 55, 314
    horses 82, 91, 189, 248
      sail 289
      wild 209
    humans 282, 296
      remote control 331
    lemurs 276
    leopards 78
    llamas 321
    mammoth, woolly 8
    marmosets 66, 254
    mastodon 45
    meerkats 320
    mice, field 202
    moles 75
    mules 152
    pigs 14, 191
      fetal 1
    rabbits 356
    raccoons 210
    rodents 219, 273
    sheep 69, 164
      desert 246
    squirrels 151, 239, 291, 365
      flying 66
      fur 135
      rocket-propelled 194
    water buffalo 51
      electric 190

animals (cont.)
  mammals (cont.)
    weasels 151, 172
      wood 241
    whales, humpback 236
    yaks, dead 230
    zebras 348
  microscopic 142
  millipede 307
  monsters, sea 262
  notebooks 161
  predators 164, 248, 285
  pterodactyl 32
  reptiles
    snakes 358
    tortoise, shells 315
  sea cucumber 215
  service 178
  slugs
    brain 36
    feral 36
  sponge, dry 62
  squid 325
    ink 325
  unicorn 289
anti-gravity 315
antidotes 244
apartment 132
appointments 68
armies, hamster 314
arrangement 54
arsenic 332
articulation 110
artifacts 77
assault 295
Asteroids 114
attacks 7, 10, 179, 299, 308
  aerial 311
attendance 58
autobiography 312
AV-8B 8
awesome 9
awesomesauce 9
axle 76

B

babies 31
back pain 116
back-pressure 2
bags, paper 244
balance 226
  cosmic 185, 201
baldness, male-pattern 233
balloon 22
banjos 287
bargain 262

bathing 212
beings, powerful 218
bike shop 2
birth 31, 257
  from eggs 313
biting 161
blades, razor 144
blimps 205
blindness 75, 179
blinking 318
blocks, psychological 272
bloodloss 134
body odor 104
body weight 94
books
  Charlotte's Web 200
  New Anatomy 54
  scripture, religious 147
  The Cat in the Hat 12
boots, work 353
botany 23
bottle rockets 153
braces, knee 354
brainwashing 21
brand loyalty 38
brands
  Apple 124
  Atari 114
  Disney 172
  Duke Nukem Forever 93
  Eeyore 172
  Flav-O-Mint 105
  Ford 68
  Frisbee 66
  Intel 124
  Jell-o 57, 310
  Kevlar 61
  Mac OS 124
  McDonnell Douglas 8
  Muppet 15
  Rubik's cube 304
  Slinky 329
  Spam 293
  Velveeta 45
  Winnie the Pooh 172
breakfast 184
breath, garlic 327
breathing 155, 201
  not 155
breeding 115
burrows 98

C

cadavers 113
  chocolate-covered 169
camouflage 44, 251

candy 38
cannibals 299
capacitors 199
car dealers 100
carbon monoxide 234
cardiac arrest 51
cards 358
cartoons 28
cartwheel 245
carving 200
casinos 324
caste 267
cataract 179
CDs 109
celebration 299
CEO 68, 105
chafing 354
chainmail 117
chainsaws 213
chairs 84
change, loose 277
chanting 37
charm 95
chasing 176
cheating 51, 324
cheese grater 362
chemicals 267
children 83, 123, 147, 223, 267, 287
choice 257
choices 268
choking 7
cholesterol, good 266
chores 253
circles 107
circumvention 224
circus 186
cities 53, 151, 338
city blocks 338
city, defense 311
clapping 87, 181, 202
cleanliness 104
climate 119
clocks 103, 130, 355
clouds 62
cocktails, Molotov 246
code 270
coercion 309
coffee breath 105
collisions 88, 327, 362
colors
  black 135, 348
  gold 147
  orange 139
  white 348
  yellow 348
coma 340
comma 260
common cold 188

communication 90, 276, 314, 365
  international 303
commuting 272
comparison 57, 61
competition 162
completion 253
concessions 101
confusion 203, 260, 282
consequences 270
conspiracy 5, 86, 234
contagions 196
control 258
conversion 214
convulsions 203
cooking 184
copyright 102
Coriolis Effect 229
cork screws 329
corrosion 236
counting 255, 324
coup 308
cover identities 259
covert 259
crack, sidewalk 4
crime 102
criticism 101
Cro-Magnon 7
crossbreeding 215
crying 267
cryptography 270
cures 212, 226, 242
curses 37
cursive 81

D

dancing 37, 158, 162, 237, 359
  jig 37, 158
darts
  blow-dart 24
  lawn darts 77
data 202, 314
data centers 314
death 15, 47, 55, 57, 107, 119, 157, 199, 206, 230, 251, 262, 289, 291, 302, 322, 328, 358, 363
  by rubber band 206
decapitation 354
deception 59
dedication 258
defecation 69
  self 158
defense 117, 118, 170
definitions 81
delays 149

dementia 212
demons 198, 270
denial 127
derailing 235
design 101, 106, 122, 143, 175, 207, 216, 336
destruction 123, 279
detoxification 290
devouring 11
dictionary 230
dimensions, parallel 245
dimes 252
diners 218
diplomacy 190
disappearance 112, 185
disappointment 147
disbelief 44
discontent 17
discovery 173, 289, 315
disfiguration 209
disphoria 212
dissolving 352
distance 214
distraction 112, 128
dizziness 229, 250
DNA 296
domestication 164
doorknobs 13
doorway, transdimensional 119
dork 126
dosages 332
doughnut shops 169
dread 207
drilling 234, 278
driving 20, 88
dunce cap 48
dunces 48
dyslexia 212

E

earthquakes 264, 347
eating 327
efficiency 70
elasticity 194
elders 287
elephantitis 172
emergency 132
endorsements 38
enemies 109, 190, 117, 220
enslavement 236
enunciation 90
equilibrium 4
escape 240
escape velocity 29
ethnicity 89

euphoria 157
evil 112, 274, 280
evils, lesser of 257
evolution 115, 215, 296
excuses 312
existence 34, 265
experiments 296
explosions 51, 131, 156, 216, 336, 338, 341
exposure 72
expressions, "third time's a charm" 95
extinction 289
extortion 102

F

facts, little known 199, 204, 311
failure 137
fairy tales 312
fake 40, 60
falling 4, 71
family 257, 267
fan 42
fanaticism 174
fashion 73, 78, 86, 126, 135, 171, 197, 324, 362, 365
  belt 171
  inside-out 219
fast-forward 42
fault lines 2
faux pas 354
fear 41, 207, 285, 294, 298
feces
  bird 13
  sheep 69
feeding 249
fencers 137
fetus 31
fighting 271
  interplanetary 309
  pit 287
filing cabinets 106
film 227
fingerpainting 188
finite values 183
fire 132, 156, 168, 193, 198, 221, 241, 246, 359
firsts 2, 6, 8, 15, 42, 46, 61, 134, 173, 193, 329, 334
flashlight 175
flight 59, 62, 66, 72, 107, 129, 132, 140, 160, 193, 205, 225, 243, 262, 326, 345, 361, 362
floating 132, 341
flocks 160

flyswatters 305
following orders 98
food 249
  apples 82
  artichokes 322
  bacon, production 121
  bananas 296
  beef 14
  burgers 14
  cabbage 346
  candy 231
  candy cane 146
  carrots 328
  cheese 14, 45, 244, 362
  cheese sticks 196
  cheeseburger 14
  chocolate 3, 281, 284
  coconut 205
  coffee 105, 186, 212, 349
  cookie 113
    as payment 150
  delicacies 288
  doughnuts 169
  eggs 184, 313
  energy bar 14
  fingers 307
  fruits 83, 231, 328
  garlic 327
  gingerbread 330
  glaze, sugar 169
  grain 178
  grapefruits 187
  gravy 294
  grenades 143
  ground beef 14
  hamburger 14
  houses 330
  ice cream 48, 323
  ice cream cone 48
  jam 261
    storage 261
  jawbreakers 30
  Jell-o 57
  jellybeans 30
  lettuce 11
  milk 204, 352
  mints 105
    coffee-flavored 105
  muffins, blueberry 337
  oatmeal 188
  onions 143
  peanut butter 39
  pickles 286
  pigeons 151
  pineapples 319
  potatoes 273, 298
    sweet 317
  prunes 18
  pudding 89

food (cont.)
  radishes 242
  raw sewage 327
  salad dressing 288
  salt 36
  sandwiches 14, 148
  sauce 9
  sausage 312
  souffle 300
  souls 292
  soup, chicken noodle 163
  Spam 293
  spices 364
  steak 238
  sugar 45
  supply 261
  surger 14
  syrup, maple 113
  tacos 364
  tea, sweet 286
  testing 296
  tomatoes 83, 101
  vegetables 83, 215, 328
    grenades 143
  vinegar 242
  waffles 353
  yams 317
food processor 126, 277
forfeit 239
forgetfulness 230
forking, accidental 141
formaldehyde 1, 32, 169
forward roll 137
fossils 283
fraud 40
frying pans 184
fur 246
furniture 216

G

galaxies 99
gambling 324
gardening 23
gas 310
gasoline 246
gelatin 139
genocide 136
geography 193
giants 77
gnomes
  garden 173, 203
  jam 261
  skin 359
goblins 198
government 118
  state 350

grammar 260, 362
gravity 29
    anti-gravity 315
gross 147
ground 258
ground cover 316
growth 189
guitar 331
gymnastics 137

H

hairballs 79
hairier 8
hallucination 145, 223
hamster wheels 55, 314
handbag 17
handsaw 120
handstand 182
happiness 183
Harrier 8
hatred 359
hats 12
    bizzare 324
    funny 32
head trauma 88
headache 240
health 163, 188, 212, 332, 354
heartbeat 191
heat 168, 184
heat exhaustion 223
heat shields 85
height 228
helium 216
helmets 365
herding 222
heredity 267
heroin 49
heroine 49
high-wire 186
history 77, 176, 220, 324, 333
    corporate 68
hive mind 31, 312
hopping 356
hotels 271
house arrest 51
houses
    as food 330
    carnivorous 256
    haunted 256
    spooky 256
humor 195
hunting 59, 82, 82, 192, 248, 285, 305
    bear 305

hurricane 146
hydrogen 156
hygiene 327
hypertension 186

I

ice 208
ideas, good 153, 247, 343
idioms 230
immunity 104, 163, 168
impersonation 15
implosion 183
impossibility 87
impostor 15
indecent exposure 102
indecision 176
independence, American 149
indigestion 159
inevitability 203
infestation 241
inflating 346
inside-out 334
insomnia 242
inspection 356
instruments, musical 157
interaction 337
intergalactic warfare 331
internet 293, 314, 321
invasion, alien 84
invention 76, 101, 106, 122, 131, 134, 213, 272, 329, 351
inversion 183
island 178

J

jars 261
jewels 297
Jiminies 360
jokes 58, 195
    practical 5
jukeboxes 336
jumping 192

K

kamikaze 243
key 119
keyboard 136, 292
keypad, numeric 292
kicking 177

kilt 73
knee braces 354
knife fight 203

L

label 23
laborers, microscopic 136
lakes, frozen 220
landmass, robotic 170
landscaping 60
language 211, 260, 273, 344
languages
    English 108, 260, 273
    Portuguese 92
    Sanskrit 300
    Swahili 344
lateness 47
laughter 303
laundry 203
lava 2
law 102, 150
lawns, front 241
laws 9
laziness 248
legend, Greek 113
lens flare 35
leopard print 78
letters 211, 212
levitation 107, 361
licking 46
life 127, 342
life vest 346
light 148
light show 162
light
    edibility 148
    speed 227
lightning 209, 258
linguistics 211
lint, dryer 30
literature 49
lithium 156
logos 35
LOL 321
loneliness 64
lotion 242
lure 241
lying 43

M

mace 165
machine, killing 120
magic 193, 245, 316

maiming 142
make-up 49
manufacturing 42, 216, 281, 290
marketing 8, 14
martial arts 363
math 87, 95, 167, 202, 214, 252, 360
   complex 326
   differential equations 252
   division 167
   poor 250
mating 151
measurement 214
   units of 360
media 19
melody 157
melting 210
memorandum 14
memory 312
metric 214
military 140
mills
   blood 175
   water 175
mind control 86, 89
mini-skirt 73
miniature 263
mining 234
misconceptions 75, 80, 109, 117, 147, 157, 310, 322, 356
mist 192
misuse 260
moire 348
money 61
monotony 242
montage 227
mops 259
mornings 265
motivation 116
mountains 71
movies
   Bill and Ted's Bogus Journey 333
   E.T. 175
   Star Wars 174
   The Three Amigos 15
multiplication 95
murder 102, 120, 358
muscle twitches 348
music 157, 162, 227
   as weaponry 221
   pop 157
   rhythm 162
mutation 257

N

names 24, 65, 91, 92
   Jeeves 254
   silly 207
nanobots 104
narcissism 262
NASA 310
national anthems 63
navigation 323
Nazi 24
needles 2
networks, underground 86
newspapers 19
night 261
nitroglycerin 364
nobility 100
notebooks
   hard-bound 161
   spiral-bound 161
nudity 96
numbers 53, 55, 56, 61, 64, 65, 67, 95, 123, 125, 129, 137, 142, 152, 165, 167, 177, 214, 270, 294, 297, 307, 323, 334, 336, 360
   even 167
   finite 340
   phone 270
   pi 360
numbness 226

O

oars 224, 264
obese 12
obesity 171
objects, large 20
obscenities 200
obstacle course 176
occupations
   assassin 363
   bartender 259
   clowns 44, 358
      rodeo 152
   cowboy 324
   dentist 211
   factory laborer 17
   farmer 86
   janitor 267
      high school 259
   landlord 150
   Marine, Icelandic 24
   mime 329
   miner, colonial 234
   ninja 363
   pilot, fighter 243

occupations (cont.)
   pirate 324
   plumber 137
   servant 79
   shoesmith 211
   student 154
      graduate 131
   teacher 12, 112, 263
   technician 334
   thief, jewel 86
oil 153
oil, motor 288, 312
opium 49
orbit 29
organizations
   Beef Production Association 14
   Board of Advisors 14
   National Elevator Test Bureau 50
orphans 284
orthodontics 131
oxygen 156

P

packs 285
pain 158
ainting 40
palindromes 111, 282
pan and scan 16
panic 348
pants 268, 342
   well-starched 140
paper 173, 188
paper mache 365
papercraft 103
parasol 142
parking decks 311
particles 249
parts, extra 276
passing out 155
paste 242
patterns 320
pauses 260
pedicures 213
pens, ballpoint 115
people
   ancient 7, 98, 173, 184
   Brutus 41
   Caesar 41
   California Raisins 18
   Caulton, Fredrick 2
   citizens, microscopic 156
   Cleveland, Grover 5
   crowds 176
   Doggs, Hugh 67

people (cont.)
- Dr. Seuss 12
- Eskimo 67
- Flemmingberg, Rupert P. 137
- Frederick 91
- Henson, Jim 15
- Holke, Arthur C. 322
- hostages 152
- Jack the Ripper 19
- Jefferson, Thomas 283
- Johnston, Remy 6
- Kingswell, James 46
- Kleetzer, Dr. Francis 211
- Lincoln, Abraham 280
- Mayans 322
- me 271
- Mongolia, children 128
- Nash, Frederick 171
- Nodleholm, Frederich 305
- nomads 115
- Norton the Creepy Guy with a Knife Behind You 19
- Nukem, Duke 93
- O'Learysmith, April 58
- prisoners of war 322
- Short, Martin 15
- Smith, Jefferson Sheldon Sumpter Cates-Ford Henderson 65
- Solo, Han 174
- Stevenson, Johnson K. 209
- Texans 365
- the Devil 143
- Titus, Sagebrush Carl 324
- tribe, Woohaka 128
- upper class 288
- VanStanzberg 54
- vegetarians 189
- veterans 298
- vocalists 157
- Von Camp, Frederich 254
- warmongers 156
- Washington, George 60
- Weinsteimer, Harold 334
- women, medieval 49
- Wright brothers 193
- Yodelman, Bob 97
- you 133

percentages 30,33,36,52,70, 129, 154,163,219,223,239,264, 269,295,296,301,304,312, 319,322,357

perception 34, 44, 71, 74, 105, 107, 177, 209, 232, 237, 348

permanence 340
pest control 320
pet 254
phone calls, long distance 303
phones 90
- cellular 72
photography 340
phrases 317
piercings 166, 331
pinball, intergalactic 99
pipes 287
pity, annual 136
places
- Africa
  - Central 347
  - Egypt 173
  - Timbuktu 154
- Asia 222
  - Gobi Desert 269
  - India 227
  - Japan 243
  - New Guinea 173
  - Siberia 190, 246
- beaches 193
- Bering Strait 3
- Central America
  - Costa Rica 223
  - Mexico 305
  - Panama 63
- Earth 34, 85, 133, 171, 255, 264, 309, 313, 358
  - core 11, 30
  - crust 2
  - re-entry 85
- Europe
  - Belgium
    - Antwerp 343
    - Brussels 343
    - Gent 343
  - Finland 97
  - Germany 24
  - Iceland 24, 25
  - Italy 121
    - Rome 41
    - Sistine Chapel 40
    - Southern 170
  - Netherlands,
    - Amsterdam 343
  - Norway 289
  - Portugal 92
- Hell, rainbow 109
- Jupiter 310
- Mediterranean Sea 170
- North America 44
  - Canada 61
  - Greenland 110
  - Southern 288

places (cont.)
- North America (cont.)
  - United States 150, 206, 283
    - Alaska 220
      - Eastern 58
    - Arizona, Tulsa 254
    - Arkansas 318, 350
    - California
      - Hollywood 16
      - Los Angeles 180
    - Illinois 184
      - Skokie 218
    - Kentucky,
      - Collinsworth 9
    - Lake Mead 6
    - Louisiana 300
    - Michigan
      - Detroit, Southern 128
      - Holland 65
    - Montana 2, 58
    - Nebraska 139, 154, 166, 209
      - Winchester 67
    - New Hampshire 171
    - Ohio, Dayton 2
    - Rhode Island 29, 165
    - Southeastern 239
    - Tennessee 150
    - Texas 365
    - Virginia, Powhatan County 151
    - Washington, Seattle 154
    - Wyoming 5
  - ocean 308
- Rangaria 98
- South America 160, 227
  - Andes Mountains 194
  - Brazil 178, 305
- southern hemisphere 229
- the Moon 309
- the Sun 309
- the universe 181, 183, 218
- underground 98
plaid 73
planets 52
- as weaponry 309
- fashion 171
- movement 138
- obesity 171
plants 11, 23
- angry 269
- cactus 269
- cocoa 169
- dandelions 251

plants (cont.)
  flowers 316
  papyrus 173
  plankton 236
  seaweed 309
  trees 200, 238
    cherry 60
  Venus flytrap 215
  weeds 251
plastic surgery 16
plastics 223
playing dead 158
poison 163, 191, 357
poop 13
possession 331
post office 204
postal system 149
potty training 147
power, animal 314
preferences 165
preservatives 169
prevention 123
prison 106
prizes, consolation 257
process 277
projectiles 322
proof, scientific 145
propeller 129
propellerhead 126
proportions 307
propulsion 289
protection 117, 168, 170, 187, 194
psychotic break 50
public drunkenness 102
punctuality 253
punctuation 90, 260
push-ups 97
pushpins 24
pyramids 101

Q

quest 297
queue 336

R

rabies 1
races, three-legged 259
radar 323
radiation
  ultraviolent 142
  ultraviolet 142
rage 159

raincoats 219
rainwater 352
ratios 30
reactions, chemical 325
reading 81, 166
realities, alternate 69
reality 279
  fabric of 237
realizations 158
reanimation 142
reconnaissance 259
records 228
recruiting 259
recursion 81, 112
recycling 353
reflection 184
refrigeration 204
regurgitation 322
rent 150
research 175, 211
reset 342
resistance 246
resources, natural 266, 274
respect 287
restaurant 216
reverse 88, 277
reversibility 219
rewind 42
ridicule 303
rites of passage 322
roach bomb 320
road trips, spontaneous 247
robots 170, 199
rockets, bottle 29
rocks, throwing 220
rocksault 221
roman candles 153
rooms, spinning 250
rope 61
rubber bands 206, 258
Rubick's cube 304
running 107, 254, 314

S

safety 132, 141, 164, 168, 187, 203, 209, 296, 328, 335
sales 105
saliva 191
saloons 324
salt, rock 221
sand 32, 188
sandstorms 269
sanity 125
saran wrap 168
sauce, awesome 9

school, elementary 112
science 145, 227, 289, 337
  anthropology 147
  archaeology 77, 147, 173
  astrophysics 138
  chemistry 156, 208, 231, 325, 337
  engineering 199
  etymology 14, 31, 81, 112, 179, 207, 221, 273, 321, 322
  physics 20, 107, 148, 183, 227, 279
    Newtonian 263
  thermodynamics 183
scuba 351
seashells 281
secrets 300
security, home 224
seeds 23, 313, 322
sentence 260
sentience 216, 217, 240
sewage, raw 281, 327
sewers 218, 334
shelter 194
shield 7
shock 27
shoelaces 134, 344
shoes 134, 144, 261, 305
  golf cleats 359
  indoor soccer 305
  soles 144
  tying 233
shooting 15, 174
shrine 147
shuttlecock 79
sidewalks 4, 251
  carnivorous 251
signs 38, 96, 250
silk 61
silverware 141
simplicity 195
sitting 347
skates, ice 144
sketchbooks 217
skills, basic 259
skin irritation 354
sky-rise 132
skylines 118
slavery 36, 236, 319
sleep 26, 34, 74, 208, 217, 302, 303
  deprivation 26, 244
slime 358
slurring 90
smell 249
smoking 287
sneeze 334
snorkel, emergency 22
snow 67, 316

soccer ball 346
society 272
soil 23
songs
   "100 Bottles of Beer on the Wall" 145
   "Camptown Races" 37, 214
   "Hamster Dance" 50
   "Row, Row, Row Your Boat" 63, 145
   "Three Blind Mice" 71
souls 109, 128, 157, 199, 231, 292, 340, 349
   as food 292
sound 202, 225
   finite 181
   low-frequency 285
   sonic bursts 285
   subsonic blast 363
   subsonics 4
space-time continuum 27, 34, 47, 260
spacebar 136
speaking 110
speed 146, 225, 227, 258, 293, 339, 350
speed of light 27
speed walking 350
spirits 37
spoilage 204
spontaneous combustion 338
sports
   100-meter dash 113
   badminton 79
   baseball 21
   choke tossing 322
   football 220
   gymnastics 221
   indoor soccer 305
   marathons 254
   Olympics 113, 221
   poker 51, 324
   pole vaulting 6
   professional 299
   racing 176
   soccer 346
   tennis 79
   tournament 6
stairs 71
staplers 357
staples 131, 295
stars 52
statistics 108, 125
steel 61, 278, 325
steering 258
stories 287
   "The 3 Billy Goats Gruff" 312
   true 114

strangulation 22, 217
strategy 203
strength 49, 61
string 153
stripes 348
studies 70, 195, 233
stupid 355
stuttering 90
subjugation 167
subteropolis 98
success 304
success, lack thereof 112
sucking 127
suffocation 22, 201, 242
sunlight 142
super 177
superfluous 211
superpowers 49, 72, 89, 235, 255
   immortality 182, 291
   mind control 319
   psychic 222
   superhuman strength 49
   telekinesis 269
   telepathy 31, 142, 331
   x-ray vision 212
supplemental 108
surgery 209
surnames 65
survey 165
survival 209, 327, 346
swarms 53
swings, chair 276
symbiosis 275
symmetry 282

T

tables 263
   wooden 218
tail-chasing 185, 279
talk, small 259
tape
   duct 61
   masking 23
tapping 205
tar 113
tardiness 47
tasks 253
   household 315
taste 286, 317
tattoos 166, 331
   temporary 86
teams 299
technology 55, 124
tectonics 194, 264, 327
television 303

temper 161
temperature regulation 289
tests, sainthood 155
text, ancient 147
theft 102
   soul 340
thesis 131
thumbtacks 25
tides, turning 211
time 148, 253, 262
   daylight savings 355
   days 74, 97, 145, 193, 232, 249, 297
      April Fool's Day 58
      Ides of March 41
   forever 56
   GMT 349
   hours 265
      noon 349
   minutes 37, 50, 166, 227, 278, 326, 333, 352
   months 41, 84, 204, 272, 313
      February 26
      June 232
   now 44
   seasons
      summer 297
      winter 316
   seconds 252, 263
   today 43, 88, 355
   years 84, 97 176 193 283 289 360
time travel 88, 103, 130, 227, 283, 342
timeframes
   1776 149
   1800s, late 2, 5, 19
   1840s 211
   1860s 112
   1930s 46, 139
   1940s 24, 139
   1950s 139, 169
   1960s 110, 223
   1980s 16, 184
   1990s 18
   4150s 283
   ancient history 147
   Industrial Revolution 315
   Jurassic 345
   medieval 49
   prehistory 7, 32
   recent 176, 272
   the future 222, 268
   the past 287
   War of 1812 99
   World War II 243
   WWII 24
timezones 349
timing 257

tires 301, 353
titanium 61, 290
toothpick 23
torture 117
touchdown 220
tourism 180
toxicity 330
trade-offs 306
traditions 220, 322
trampling 209
training, intense 259
transcendence 71
transit 2
   jungle 80
   public 70
translation 230, 273, 344
transportation 178, 180, 350
trapeze 298
trapezoids 241
trauma 272
travel 70, 180, 220, 247, 258, 271, 339, 343
   by cannon 272
   interstellar 335
   transdimensional 283
   work 247
tree bucket 207
trespassing 102
trials 322
tribes 121, 198, 222
true story 200
turf, artificial 138
turning 252
typing 125, 136, 326
typo 14

U

U. S. Army 259
U. S. Constitution 283
understatement 147
underwater 6
undo 342
uniqueness, lack thereof 94
units 214
upside-down 48, 54

V

VCR 42
vegetable slicer 126
vehicles 335
   airplanes 2, 8
      747 airliner 290, 339
   balloons, hot air 346

vehicles (cont.)
   cars 20, 88, 130, 160, 223
   kayak 335
   race cars 323
   roller coasters 244
   rollerblades 122
   spacecraft 282
   subterranean 2
   trains 235, 327, 343
      wrecks 209, 344
   trucks, ice cream 128, 323
venom 191
video tape 16
villains 128
violence 22, 142, 262, 285, 336
visual effects 35
vitamin C 274
volatility 341
volcanoes 2
vote 58

##

waiting 84
waking 349
walking 195, 356
   speed 350
wallpaper 40
water 62, 156, 165, 208, 215, 229
   distilled 210
   rain 352
weaponry 8, 24, 101, 109, 117, 202
   aircraft
      bombers 311, 313
      fighters 313
   artillery 308
   bombs, roaches 320
   cannonballs 101
   cannons 272
   cars, as projectiles 311
   firearms 141
   flame thrower 246
   grenades 234
   guitar 331
   islands as 170
   knives 168
   missiles, long range 311
   music as 221
   planets 309
   slingshots 70
   soap as 203
   spears, microscopic 198
   tanks, Abrams 252

weaponry (cont.)
   trebuchet 207
weight 160, 228, 294
wheel 76, 272
willpower 361
wind 42
window 132
winter 184
wishing 52
wool 164
words 108, 177
world domination 83, 297
writing 90, 177

X

There is no X

Y

yo-yo 6

Z

zero, absolute 183
zipper 17
zombies 256, 302, 349
zoos 38

www.ingramcontent.com/pod-product-compliance
Lightning Source LLC
Chambersburg PA
CBHW021138080526
44588CB00008B/106